HOW TO BECOME AIRBNB SUPERHOST IN 3 MONTHS

X GARZÓN G
AIRBNB SUPERHOST

TABLE OF CONTENTS

Introduction	5
What will you learn?	9
Understanding the Superhost Criteria	11
Perfecting Your Listing	17
Providing Exceptional Guest Experience	27
Managing Your Listings Effectively	35
Conclusion	41
Invitation to Join Airbnb	43

INTRODUCTION

Welcome to "How to Become an Airbnb Superhost in 3 Months." My name is Xiomara, and I'm delighted to share my journey and the strategies that helped me achieve Superhost status in a remarkably short time.

When I started hosting on Airbnb in 2022, I had no prior experience in the hospitality industry. Yet, within just three months, I earned the Superhost badge, a testament to my commitment and passion for providing exceptional guest experiences.

Over the past years, my Airbnb journey has been both challenging and rewarding. Hosting my house," I've garnered more than 143 reviews and maintained an impressive 4.95-star rating.

www.airbnb.co.uk/r/xiomarag759

These achievements are not just numbers but reflect the positive experiences of guests who have stayed at my property. I've learned a great deal through trial and error, and now, I want to share this knowledge to help new hosts navigate their way to success.

My Journey

Starting as an Airbnb host can be daunting. When I listed my property, I was overwhelmed by the multitude of tasks and the high expectations. I had to figure out how to attract guests, manage bookings, ensure cleanliness, handle communications, and much more. It was a steep learning curve, but with perseverance and a willingness to adapt, I quickly found my footing.

One of the first lessons I learned was the importance of standing out in a competitive market. By perfecting my listing, offering unique touches, and consistently providing top-notch service, I was able to attract more guests and earn high ratings. My journey wasn't without its bumps, but each challenge taught me valuable lessons that contributed to my success.

Why This Book?

The purpose of this book is to make your journey to becoming a Superhost as smooth and straightforward as possible. Whether you're a new host or looking to improve your hosting game, the insights and strategies I share are designed to help you succeed. In this book, you will find practical advice on every aspect of hosting, from setting up your listing and managing bookings to providing exceptional guest experiences and handling challenges.

www.airbnb.co.uk/r/xiomarag759

I'll guide you through the steps I took to achieve Superhost status and maintain it over the years. Each chapter is filled with actionable tips that you can implement immediately to improve your hosting.

www.airbnb.co.uk/r/xiomarag759

WHAT WILL YOU LEARN?

- Understanding the Superhost Criteria: Detailed breakdown of what it takes to become a Superhost.
- Perfecting Your Listing: How to create an attractive and accurate listing that stands out.
- Providing Exceptional Guest Experience: Tips for ensuring your guests have a memorable stay.
- Managing Your Listings Effectively: Tools and techniques to keep your operations running smoothly.

My Promise to You

Achieving Superhost status is more than just a badge; it's a recognition of your dedication to hospitality. My promise is to equip you with the knowledge and tools you need to reach this milestone and sustain it.

www.airbnb.co.uk/r/xiomarag759

By following the guidance in this book, you will be well on your way to becoming an exceptional host who not only meets but exceeds guest expectations.

So, are you ready to embark on this journey? Let's transform your Airbnb hosting experience and unlock the full potential of your property. With dedication, attention to detail, and the right strategies, you can achieve Superhost status in just three months.

Thank you for joining me on this journey. Let's get started!

www.airbnb.co.uk/r/xiomarag759

UNDERSTANDING THE SUPERHOST CRITERIA

Becoming an Airbnb Superhost is a prestigious achievement that signifies excellence in hosting. Superhosts are recognized for their outstanding hospitality, reliability, and dedication to providing great guest experiences. To become a Superhost, Airbnb has set specific criteria that hosts must meet consistently. This chapter will break down each criterion, explain why it's important, and provide strategies to help you meet and exceed these requirements.

Criteria 1 - Host at Least 10 Trips or Have 3 Reservations Totaling 100 Nights. The number of trips you host demonstrates your experience and ability to handle different guest situations. By hosting multiple trips, you show that you can consistently provide a high level of service.

Strategies to Achieve This:

Maximize Your Availability: Open your calendar as much as possible to increase the chances of bookings. Consider allowing instant booking to attract more guests quickly.

Promote Your Listing: Share your Airbnb link on social media, local community boards, and travel forums. Consider collaborating with local businesses to cross-promote your property.

Competitive Pricing: Research similar listings in your area and set competitive prices. Offering introductory discounts can also attract your first few bookings quickly.

Offer Unique Experiences: Highlight unique aspects of your property or location to attract guests. This could be proximity to attractions, unique amenities, or special experiences.

www.airbnb.co.uk/r/xiomarag759

Criteria 2 - Maintain a High Response Rate (90% or higher) A high response rate shows that you are attentive and responsive to potential guests, which is crucial for providing excellent customer service. Airbnb requires hosts to respond to 90% of new messages within 24 hours.

Strategies to Achieve This:

Enable Notifications: Ensure that you have notifications enabled on your phone and email so you don't miss any messages from guests.

Use Automated Responses: Set up automated responses for common questions and booking confirmations. This can help maintain your response rate even when you're busy.

www.airbnb.co.uk/r/xiomarag759

Set Realistic Expectations:
Communicate your response times in your listing description and welcome messages. Let guests know if there will be delays in response due to time zone differences or other commitments.

Criteria 3 - Maintain a 1% cancellation rate (1 cancellation per 100 reservations) or lower. A low cancellation rate is crucial for reliability. Guests need to trust that their reservations will not be canceled unexpectedly. Airbnb allows less than 1% of reservations to be canceled, with exceptions for extenuating circumstances.

Strategies to Achieve This:

Avoid Overbooking: Keep your calendar updated and avoid double-booking by syncing it with other platforms if you list your property elsewhere.

www.airbnb.co.uk/r/xiomarag759

Set Realistic Expectations: Be transparent about your property and house rules to prevent cancellations due to misunderstandings. Clear communication can prevent issues that might lead to cancellations.

Handle Issues Promptly: If a problem arises that might lead to a cancellation, communicate with the guest immediately and try to find a solution. Offering alternatives, such as a later date or a nearby property, can often resolve the issue without cancelling.

Plan for Emergencies: Have a backup plan in case of emergencies. For example, if something breaks, have a list of nearby repair services that can respond quickly.

www.airbnb.co.uk/r/xiomarag759

Criteria 4 - Receive High Overall Ratings. Guest reviews are a critical factor in maintaining Superhost status. You need to maintain a 4.8 overall rating, which reflects the quality of your property and the experience you provide.

Strategies to Achieve This:
Provide Excellent Hospitality: Ensure that every guest feels welcome and valued. Greet them personally if possible, and provide a welcome basket with snacks and a handwritten note.
Maintain Cleanliness: A clean property is one of the top factors in guest satisfaction. Hire a professional cleaning service if needed, and perform regular deep cleanings.
Offer High-Quality Amenities: Invest in comfortable bedding and well-equipped kitchen facilities. Small touches like providing coffee, tea, and local guides can enhance the guest experience.

www.airbnb.co.uk/r/xiomarag759

Request Feedback: Encourage guests to leave reviews by providing exceptional service and gently reminding them at check-out.

Understanding and meeting Airbnb's Superhost criteria requires dedication and strategic planning. By focusing on hosting multiple trips, maintaining a high response rate, receiving excellent reviews, and minimizing cancellations, you can achieve and maintain Superhost status. This chapter has provided a foundation for the specific actions you can take to meet these criteria. In the following chapters, we will delve deeper into each aspect of hosting, offering detailed strategies and tips to ensure you not only meet but exceed these standards, providing a memorable experience for every guest.

www.airbnb.co.uk/r/xiomarag759

Request Feedback: Encourage guests to leave reviews by providing exceptional service and gently reminding them at check-out.

Understanding and meeting Airbnb's Superhost criteria requires dedication and strategic planning. By focusing on hosting multiple trips, maintaining a high response rate, receiving excellent reviews, and minimizing cancellations, you can achieve and maintain Superhost status. This chapter has provided a foundation for the specific actions you can take to meet these criteria. In the following chapters, we will delve deeper into each aspect of hosting, offering detailed strategies and tips to ensure you not only meet but exceed these standards, providing a memorable experience for every guest.

www.airbnb.co.uk/r/xiomarag759

PERFECTING YOUR LISTING

Your Airbnb listing is your primary tool for attracting potential guests. A well-crafted listing not only showcases your property but also sets the tone for the type of experience guests can expect. In this chapter, we will explore how to create an irresistible title and description, take high-quality photos, write accurate and detailed descriptions, and set competitive pricing. By perfecting your listing, you can significantly increase your bookings and attract the right guests.

Craft an Irresistible Title and Description
The title of your listing is the first thing potential guests see, so it needs to be catchy, descriptive, and informative. Here are some tips to create a compelling title.

www.airbnb.co.uk/r/xiomarag759

Be Specific and Descriptive: Highlight key features that make your property stand out. For example, "Cozy Cottage Near the Peak District with Scenic Views" is more appealing than "Nice Cottage."

Use Keywords: Think about what potential guests might search for. Include words like "luxury," "spacious," "central," or "near [local attraction]."

-**Highlight Unique Selling Points**: If your property has unique features like a hot tub, fireplace, or proximity to popular attractions, mention them in the title.

Examples:
"Charming Lakefront Cabin with Private Dock"
"Modern Downtown Apartment with Rooftop Pool"
"Rustic Mountain Retreat Near Hiking Trails"

www.airbnb.co.uk/r/xiomarag759

Writing an Engaging Description Your description should paint a vivid picture of your property and what guests can expect. Here's how to make it compelling:

Start with a Strong Introduction: Capture the reader's attention with a brief overview of what makes your property special. For example, "Welcome to our serene lakefront cabin, a perfect escape from the hustle and bustle of city life."

Highlight Key Features: Describe the main attractions of your property, such as the number of bedrooms, type of beds, bathrooms, kitchen amenities, living areas, and outdoor spaces.

Mention Unique Aspects: If your property has unique features like a historic background, artistic decor, or eco-friendly amenities, be sure to include them.

www.airbnb.co.uk/r/xiomarag759

Describe the Neighbourhood: Provide information about the local area, nearby attractions, restaurants, public transport, and any special events.

Set Expectations: Be clear about house rules, check-in/check-out times, and any other important details.

Example:

Welcome to our charming lakefront cabin, a perfect retreat for families and couples. Enjoy breathtaking views of the lake from our spacious deck, cozy up by the wood-burning fireplace, and take advantage of our fully equipped kitchen. With three bedrooms and two bathrooms, our cabin comfortably accommodates up to six guests. Located just a short drive from hiking trails and local wineries, you'll find plenty of activities to enjoy during your stay."

www.airbnb.co.uk/r/xiomarag759

High-Quality Photos

High-quality photos are crucial for making a great first impression. They give potential guests a visual representation of your property and can significantly influence their decision to book.

Tips for Taking Great Photos:

Use Good Lighting: Natural light is best. Take photos during the day when your property is well-lit.

Clean and Stage Your Space: Make sure your property is spotless and decluttered. Arrange furniture and decor to make spaces look inviting and functional.

Showcase Key Areas: Include photos of all important areas, such as the living room, kitchen, bedrooms, bathrooms, and any unique features like a garden or balcony.

www.airbnb.co.uk/r/xiomarag759

Highlight Unique Features: If you have a beautiful view, a cozy fireplace, or a luxurious bathroom, make sure to highlight these in your photos.

Consider Professional Photography: Investing in professional photos can be worthwhile, especially if your property is in a competitive market.

Photo Checklist:

-Exterior shot of the property
-Living room from multiple angles
-Kitchen with focus on appliances and seating areas
-Each bedroom, showing the bed and any additional furniture
-Bathrooms, highlighting cleanliness and amenities
-Any unique or special features (e.g., hot tub, view, garden)
-Common areas like dining room or patio

www.airbnb.co.uk/r/xiomarag759

Accurate and Detailed Descriptions

An accurate and detailed description ensures that guests know exactly what to expect, which can lead to better reviews and fewer cancellations.

Key Elements of a Detailed Description:

-Property Layout: Clearly explain the layout of your property, including the number of rooms, types of beds, and any additional sleeping arrangements like sofa beds.

-Amenities: List all the amenities you offer, such as Wi-Fi, TV, kitchen appliances, laundry facilities, air conditioning, heating, and any extras like board games or books.

-House Rules: Include any important rules such as no smoking, no pets, or quiet hours.

www.airbnb.co.uk/r/xiomarag759

-Check-In/Check-Out Details: Provide information on the check-in and check-out process, including times and any specific instructions.
-Local Attractions and Accessibility: Describe nearby attractions, public transport options, and how easy it is to access your property.

Example:

"Our cozy cabin features an open-plan living area with a comfortable sofa, a wood-burning fireplace, and a flat-screen TV. The fully equipped kitchen includes a stove, refrigerator, microwave, and coffee maker, making it easy to prepare your favorite meals. The master bedroom has a queen-size bed, while the second bedroom has two twin beds. The bathroom is stocked with fresh towels and toiletries. Enjoy our large deck with a barbecue grill and outdoor seating, perfect for enjoying the sunset over the lake."

www.airbnb.co.uk/r/xiomarag759

4. Competitive Pricing

Setting the right price for your listing is crucial for attracting bookings while maximizing your revenue. Here's how to set competitive pricing:

Research Comparable Listings
- Local Market Analysis: Look at similar properties in your area to see what they charge. Consider factors like location, size, amenities, and seasonal demand.
- Adjust for Unique Features: If your property offers something unique (e.g., a prime location, special amenities), you can justify a higher price.

Dynamic Pricing
- Seasonal Pricing: Adjust your prices based on the season. High-demand periods like holidays, local events, and peak tourist seasons should have higher rates.

www.airbnb.co.uk/r/xiomarag759

- Length of Stay Discounts: Offer discounts for longer stays to attract guests looking for extended accommodations.
- Last-Minute Discounts: Consider offering discounts for last-minute bookings to fill vacant dates.

Tools and Automation
-Pricing Tools: Use dynamic pricing tools like Airbnb's Smart Pricing or third-party services like Beyond Pricing or PriceLabs to automatically adjust your rates based on market demand.
- Special Offers: Periodically offer special deals or discounts to boost occupancy during slower periods.

Example Pricing Strategy:
"Set your base rate by researching similar listings in your area. For example, if comparable properties are listed at $150 per night, consider setting your rate slightly lower at $140 to attract initial bookings.

www.airbnb.co.uk/r/xiomarag759

During peak season, increase your rate to $180. Offer a 10% discount for stays longer than a week and a 20% discount for monthly bookings. Use Airbnb's Smart Pricing tool to adjust your rates dynamically."

Perfecting your listing is a fundamental step in becoming a successful Airbnb host. A well-crafted title and description, high-quality photos, accurate and detailed descriptions, and competitive pricing will help you attract more guests and set the stage for positive reviews. In the following chapters, we will delve deeper into providing exceptional guest experiences and managing your listings effectively to ensure your success as an Airbnb host.

www.airbnb.co.uk/r/xiomarag759

PROVIDING EXCEPTIONAL GUEST EXPERIENCE

Creating an exceptional guest experience is at the heart of becoming a successful Airbnb host. Happy guests are more likely to leave positive reviews, recommend your property to others, and return for future stays. This chapter will explore the key elements of providing an outstanding guest experience: effective communication, ensuring cleanliness and comfort, adding thoughtful touches, and being a local guide.

1. Communication is Key

Effective communication is crucial for setting the right expectations and ensuring a smooth experience for your guests.

www.airbnb.co.uk/r/xiomarag759

Respond Promptly and Politely

Timely Responses: Aim to respond to inquiries and booking requests within a few hours, preferably within 24 hours. Prompt responses show that you are attentive and committed to providing great service.

Professionalism: Always communicate politely and professionally. Address guests by their names and answer their questions thoroughly.

Use Templates: Create templates for common messages, such as booking confirmations, check-in instructions, and thank-you notes. This saves time and ensures consistency.

Provide Clear Check-In Instructions

Detailed Directions: Give clear and detailed directions to your property. Include landmarks, GPS coordinates, and public transport options if applicable.

www.airbnb.co.uk/r/xiomarag759

Check-In Procedures: Explain the check-in process, including where to find the keys, any codes needed for entry, and specific instructions for accessing the property.

Be Available: Let your guests know how they can reach you if they have any questions or issues during their stay. Being accessible can prevent small problems from becoming major inconveniences.

2. Cleanliness and Comfort

Cleanliness and comfort are top priorities for guests. A spotless and comfortable property can significantly enhance their stay.

Ensure Your Property is Spotless

Professional Cleaning: Consider hiring a professional cleaning service to ensure your property is thoroughly cleaned between guests.

www.airbnb.co.uk/r/xiomarag759

Pay attention to high-touch areas like doorknobs, light switches, and remote controls.

Regular Inspections: Conduct regular inspections to ensure that everything is in order. Look for maintenance issues, wear and tear, and cleanliness.

Stock Cleaning Supplies: Provide guests with basic cleaning supplies like disinfectant wipes, paper towels, and trash bags. This helps them keep the space clean during their stay.

Provide Quality Linens, Towels, and Toiletries

Comfortable Bedding: Invest in high-quality mattresses, pillows, and bedding. Clean and comfortable beds are often mentioned in positive reviews.

Fresh Towels: Offer plenty of fresh towels and washcloths. Consider providing different sizes for various needs.

www.airbnb.co.uk/r/xiomarag759

Toiletries: Stock basic toiletries such as shampoo, conditioner, body wash, and hand soap.

3. Thoughtful Touches

Small, thoughtful touches can make a big difference in how guests perceive their stay.

Welcome Note or Small Gift

Personalized Note: Leave a handwritten welcome note for your guests. It's a simple gesture that shows you care about their stay.

Small Gifts: Consider providing a small gift, such as a local treat. This can create a memorable first impression.

Stock Basic Necessities
Snacks and Beverages: Stock the kitchen with basic necessities like coffee, tea, bottled water, and snacks.

www.airbnb.co.uk/r/xiomarag759

This is especially appreciated by guests who arrive late or have had a long journey.

Essentials: Ensure that your kitchen has essential items like salt, pepper, oil, and basic cooking utensils. This makes it easier for guests to prepare meals.

4. Be a Local Guide

Helping your guests navigate the local area can greatly enhance their experience and make their stay more enjoyable.

Recommendations for Local Attractions, Restaurants, and Activities

Personal Favorites: Share your favorite local spots, such as restaurants, cafes, parks, and attractions. Guests appreciate insider tips that they might not find in guidebooks.

www.airbnb.co.uk/r/xiomarag759

Variety: Offer a variety of recommendations to suit different interests and budgets. Include options for families, couples, and solo travelers.

Updated Information: Ensure your recommendations are up-to-date. Regularly check to make sure the places you recommend are still open and maintain their quality.

Provide Maps and Brochures

Local Maps: Provide maps of the local area, including public transportation routes and nearby points of interest.

Brochures and Guides: Collect brochures and guides from local tourist information centers. Leave these in an accessible place for your guests.

Custom Guidebook: Create a custom guidebook with detailed information about your property, local attractions, dining options, and transportation. I

www.airbnb.co.uk/r/xiomarag759

nclude emergency contact information and house rules.

Providing an exceptional guest experience involves more than just offering a place to stay. By focusing on effective communication, maintaining cleanliness and comfort, adding thoughtful touches, and serving as a local guide, you can create memorable experiences that encourage positive reviews and repeat bookings. In the next chapter, we will explore how to manage your listings effectively to ensure smooth operations and maximize your success as an Airbnb host.

www.airbnb.co.uk/r/xiomarag759

MANAGING YOUR LISTINGS EFFECTIVELY

Effective management of your Airbnb listings is essential for maintaining high standards and ensuring a seamless experience for both you and your guests. This chapter will cover the importance of automation, staying organized, and soliciting and responding to feedback.

1. Automate Where Possible
Automation can save you time and reduce the risk of human error, allowing you to focus on providing an excellent guest experience.

Use Automated Messaging
-Booking Confirmations: Set up automated messages to confirm bookings. Include important information such as check-in instructions, house rules, and contact details.

www.airbnb.co.uk/r/xiomarag759

Check-In Instructions: Automate messages with detailed check-in instructions sent a few days before arrival.

Follow-Up Messages: Schedule messages to check in with guests after their first night to ensure everything is going well and to remind them to leave a review after their stay.

Employ a Pricing Tool

Dynamic Pricing: Use dynamic pricing tools like Airbnb's Smart Pricing or third-party services such as Beyond Pricing or PriceLabs. These tools adjust your rates based on market demand, local events, and seasonal trends, helping you stay competitive.

2. Stay Organized

Staying organized is crucial for managing multiple bookings, cleaning schedules, and maintenance tasks efficiently.

www.airbnb.co.uk/r/xiomarag759

Keep a Calendar

Track Bookings: Maintain a calencar to track all your bookings, ensuring you never double-book or miss a reservation.

Sync Calendars: If you list your property on multiple platforms, use a channel manager to sync your calendars and prevent double bookings.

Schedule Cleanings: Coordinate cleaning schedules to ensure your property is ready for the next guest. Consider using a cleaning service with a calendar integration to streamline this process.

Have a Checklist for Turnovers
Turnover Checklist: Create a detailed checklist for turnovers to ensure nothing is missed during the cleaning and preparation process.

www.airbnb.co.uk/r/xiomarag759

Include tasks such as laundering linens, restocking supplies, and checking for damages.

Inspection: Perform a quick inspection after each cleaning to ensure the property meets your standards.

3. Solicit and Respond to Feedback

Guest feedback is invaluable for improving your service and maintaining a high rating.

Encourage Guests to Leave Reviews

Positive Reinforcement: Gently remind guests to leave a review after their stay. Explain how reviews help you improve your service and assist future guests in making informed decisions.

Review Request Messages: Send a follow-up message thanking guests for their stay and encouraging them to share their experience in a review.

www.airbnb.co.uk/r/xiomarag759

Address Negative Reviews: Respond to negative reviews professionally and constructively. Acknowledge any issues, apologize sincerely, and explain what steps you're taking to resolve them. This shows potential guests that you are attentive and committed to improving.

Managing your listings effectively is key to running a successful Airbnb business. By automating routine tasks, staying organized, and actively soliciting and responding to feedback, you can maintain high standards and ensure a smooth operation. In the next chapter, we will discuss handling challenges, from dealing with difficult guests to maintaining your property and handling cancellations.

www.airbnb.co.uk/r/xiomarag759

CONCLUSION

Congratulations on reaching the end of "How to Become an Airbnb Superhost in 3 Months"! By now, you should have a comprehensive understanding of what it takes to achieve and maintain Superhost status.

Becoming a Superhost is just the beginning. Maintaining this status requires ongoing dedication and a commitment to continuous improvement. Keep abreast of changes in Airbnb policies, stay informed about market trends, and always look for ways to enhance your guest experience.

Remember, the key to success lies in the details.

www.airbnb.co.uk/r/xiomarag759

From the moment a potential guest views your listing to the time they check out, every interaction counts. Strive for excellence in all aspects of your hosting journey.

Thank you for embarking on this journey with me. I hope the insights and strategies shared in this book will help you achieve your goal of becoming an Airbnb Superhost in just three months. Here's to your success and many happy guests!

Happy Hosting!

Xiomara

www.airbnb.co.uk/r/xiomarag759

INVITATION FROM XIOMARA

Hello Future Hosts,

I'm Xiomara, and I'm thrilled to share my journey with you. When I started hosting on Airbnb in 2022, I had no experience and plenty of uncertainty. Yet, within just three months, I achieved Superhost status! Today, with over 143 reviews and an impressive 4.95-star rating, I've learned what it takes to succeed on this platform. Now, I want to help you achieve the same success.

Are you ready to transform your space into a thriving rental and start earning extra income? Joining Airbnb is a fantastic opportunity to share your home with guests from all over the world while creating memorable experiences.

www.airbnb.co.uk/r/xiomarag759

Why Join Airbnb?
- Extra Income: Turn your space into a profitable venture.
- Flexibility: Rent out your space on your own terms.
-Community: Join a supportive network of hosts worldwide.
-Personal Growth: Enhance your hospitality skills and meet amazing people.

By using my referral link, you'll receive special benefits to kickstart your hosting experience.

https://www.airbnb.co.uk/r/xiomarag759

www.ingramcontent.com/pod-product-compliance
Lightning Source LLC
Chambersburg PA
CBHW050246230526
45470CB00005B/2135